The Rise of Modern China

Tony Allan

www.heinemann.co.uk
Visit our website to find out more information about Heinemann Library books.

To order:
 Phone 44 (0) 1865 888066
Send a fax to 44 (0) 1865 314091
 Visit the Heinemann Bookshop at www.heinemann.co.uk to browse our catalogue and order online.

First published in Great Britain by Heinemann Library,
Halley Court, Jordan Hill, Oxford OX2 8EJ,
a division of Reed Educational and Professional Publishing Ltd.
Heinemann is a registered trademark of Reed Educational and Professional Publishing Ltd.

OXFORD MELBOURNE AUCKLAND
JOHANNESBURG BLANTYRE GABORONE
IBADAN PORTSMOUTH (NH) USA CHICAGO

Produced for Heinemann Library by Discovery Books Limited
Designed by Ian Winton
Editor: Rebecca Hunter
Consultant: John Chinnery
Illustrated by Stefan Chabluk
Originated by Dot Gradations
Printed by Wing King Tong in Hong Kong

ISBN 0 431 11994 5 (hardback)
06 05 04 03
10 9 8 7 6 5 4 3 2

ISBN 0 431 11999 6 (paperback)
06 05 04 03
10 9 8 7 6 5 4 3 2 1

British Library Cataloguing in Publication Data
Allan, Tony, 1946 –
    The rise of modern China. – (20th century perspectives)
    1.China – History – 20th century – Juvenile literature
    2.China – Social conditions – 1949– – Juvenile literature
    I.Title
    951'.05

Acknowledgements
The publishers would like to thank the following for permission to reproduce photographs:
Camera Press London pp. 23, 25, 30, 36; Chris Fairclough Photography pp. 4, 41, 42, 43; Corbis 8, pp. 11, 32, 37, 38, 39, 40; Hulton Archive pp. 24, 29, 34; Hulton Deutsch Collection pp. 15, 17; Hulton Getty pp. 5, 7, 10, 28, 31, 35; Peter Newark's Historical Pictures pp. 9, 22, 27, 33; Peter Newark's Military Pictures pp. 6, 13, 16, 18, 19; Peter Newark's Pictures pp. 12, 20, 21, 26

Cover photograph reproduced with permission of Peter Newark's Military Pictures.

Every effort has been made to contact copyright holders of any material reproduced in this book. Any omissions will be rectified in subsequent printings if notice is given to the publishers.

Any words appearing in the text in bold, **like this**, are explained in the glossary.

Contents

The end of the emperors

For China, the 19th century was a time of disasters. For long periods in its past the nation had led the world, but by 1900 it had reached a low point.

By then its history already stretched back over almost 4000 years. For more than half that time it had been united under the rule of emperors who called their realm the Middle Kingdom, for they thought it was the centre of the world. People not fortunate enough to be their subjects were barbarians. Outsiders were occasionally permitted to visit the Emperor, but only to pay tribute. To show respect visitors had to **kowtow**, kneeling on all fours to touch their foreheads to the floor before the imperial throne.

Leading the world

For much of China's history, the country's rulers had reason for their pride. China was a world beater. Paper, printing, cast iron, gunpowder, porcelain, paper money, the magnetic compass – all were Chinese inventions.

Literature, art and philosophy were important in China at a time when many Western peoples were still living in grass and mud huts. The nation also achieved great feats of engineering, notably the Great Wall, built to keep out hostile neighbours more than 2200 years ago.

By the mid-19th century, little was left of China's glorious past. The ruling Qing dynasty was of foreign origin, established in the 17th century by invaders from **Manchuria** to the north. Its early rulers had been effective, but their successors were less so. The country whose technology had once led the world had gradually fallen behind.

A land of peasants

At a time when the Industrial Revolution was transforming the West, China remained a land of peasants. Where the Western nations had railways and steamships, the Chinese still used oxen and traditional sailing boats, called junks. In the countryside, most of those who worked the land did not own it. Instead, they rented plots from landowners who often demanded half of all they grew as rent. Seeing China's weakness, other nations stepped in to take advantage. During the 19th century China fought and lost two wars against the British, who took up arms to protect their trade in opium. As the price of victory, Britain demanded huge payments to cover the costs of the war. They also insisted on special privileges for British merchants and took control of the island of Hong Kong, off China's southern coast.

The unequal treaties

After China's defeat in the Opium Wars, other powers including France, the United States, Russia and Germany all demanded special privileges for their own traders. These countries were duly granted special trading rights in the **'unequal treaties'**, signed by the Chinese government under threat of force.

Slum-dwellers squat in an earth-floored shack in 1871. The photographer, a Scot named John Thompson, wrote that he had never seen 'poverty so wretched, ignorance so intense' as in China at that time.

The final humiliation came in the 1890s, when China found itself at war with its Asian neighbour, Japan. The dispute centred on influence in the independent kingdom of Korea, traditionally a **tributary state** of China. Although much smaller than China in land and population, Japan had modernized its army and its economy along Western lines. When its forces defeated the Chinese, first on land and then at sea, China's weakness was obvious for all to see. Once the hub of the world, it was now no longer the chief power even in its own region.

The root of the problem

At the root of China's problems in the 19th century was a population explosion. The number of Chinese had almost tripled in 100 years, from 143 million in 1741 to 413 million by 1840, but food supplies had failed to keep up: the amount of rice – the nation's staple crop – available per person had virtually halved. The result was famine whenever there was a bad harvest. The famine of 1877-78 claimed five million lives.

Revolution!

Poverty-stricken and humiliated, the Chinese people resorted to violence. In 1900, after the nation's defeat by the Japanese, gangs of youths, fanatically dedicated to restoring the nation's honour, joined an underground revolutionary movement known as the Society of the Righteous and Harmonious Fists. The Boxers, as the rebels became known, practised a secret form of martial arts that they claimed could magically protect them from bullets. Directing their anger against everything foreign, they took control of Beijing, laying siege to the embassy compound where diplomats from all the leading powers of the day had taken refuge. When the imperial government not only failed to stop the Boxers, and even secretly lent it support, eight nations, including the British, Americans, Germans, French, Russians and Japanese, sent troops to put it down – the only time the great powers of the day had combined in such a way.

The real ruler

The crushing of the Boxers by foreign troops was a final humiliation for the imperial system. By that time real power rested not in the hands of the Emperor himself, but with the ageing Empress Dowager. In face of all the disasters afflicting the country, she stubbornly resisted any policy changes that would lessen her powers. In her iron grip, the imperial court's last chances to change and survive ended. Then, in November 1908, she and the then-emperor died on successive days. Pu-yi, the heir to the throne, was only two years old. The fate of the Qing dynasty was sealed.

Sun Zhongshan

Even then, the imperial tradition took three more years to end. The man who eventually brought the dynasty down was from southern China and named Sun

*A painting by a Western artist shows an international force fighting during the **Boxer Rebellion** in 1901. The Boxers had risen up against the foreign powers who had taken advantage of China's weakness to seize territory and special privileges from its government.*

Zhongshan (also spelt Sun Yat-sen). Born into a peasant family, he had spent part of his childhood in Hawaii and had then studied medicine in the British colony of Hong Kong, where he became familiar with Western ways. After trying and failing to get a job in the imperial administration, he became convinced that the only hope for China was to get rid of the emperors altogether and establish a **Republic**. From 1894 on he devoted himself to that goal, spending most of the time as an **exile** in Britain, the United States, and Japan.

The tenth uprising

Between 1895 and 1910, Sun's Republicans made nine attempts to start a revolution in China. All failed. But in 1911 they tried for a tenth time. This time, crucially, the spark was struck by unhappy units of the Chinese army, which captured the central city of Wuhan – the rebels' first real military success.

That one victory was enough to cause the collapse of the entire imperial system. Over the next two months, virtually the entire country rose up, declaring decisively for the Republic. The advisers to the Emperor – still only five years old – realized Pu-yi would have to abdicate, and on 1 January 1912, the Republic of China was officially proclaimed, with Sun Zhongshan as its first president. Two thousand years of imperial rule had come to an end.

Aged 45, Sun Zhongshan stares at the camera in 1912, months after the revolution that he had inspired had swept away the Qing dynasty and brought an end to more than 2000 years of imperial rule.

Sun's London adventure

Sun Zhongshan's first attempt to overthrow the government, in 1895 when he was 29 years old, was a dismal failure, and he was forced to go into exile to avoid arrest. Abroad, his activities continued to attract the attention of the Chinese authorities. In London in 1896 he was kidnapped and imprisoned in the Chinese embassy. He would almost certainly have been killed if he had not managed to smuggle out a message addressed to his former tutor, a well-known English surgeon. The surgeon contacted Britain's Foreign Office, which used its influence to get Sun released.

A time of troubles

As China's first president, Sun quickly realized that getting rid of the Qing dynasty was the easy part of the job. The harder task was to find an alternative form of government. For over 2000 years imperial rule had been the cement binding the nation together. Its abolition created a gap at the centre of power that Sun himself did not have the power or influence to fill. He was forced to step aside after only 47 days to make way for a former war minister, Yuan Shikai. Sun did this in the hope of securing a new future for China, but he was quickly disappointed. It soon became apparent that Yuan had no great interest in democracy, the cause that Sun had fought for. Instead, Yuan first set out to rule as a military dictator and then took steps to have himself declared emperor.

Yuan died unexpectedly in 1916 before he could become emperor. When he died, China fell apart. Local military commanders across the nation seized power in their own regions. Opposition was ruthlessly suppressed, and central authority all but disappeared.

The 4th May Movement

In the big cities, there was still support for reform and national revival. On 4 May 1919, 3000 students demonstrated in Beijing against the peace treaty ending World War I, which had transferred most of defeated Germany's trading rights in China not to the Chinese themselves, but rather to the Japanese, who had fought on the winning side. Although the demonstrators had no power to change events, their appeal to national feeling was popular. In the south, too, Sun Zhongshan was struggling to keep the **Nationalist** cause alive. He set up two short-lived governments in the city of Guangzhou with the help of local **warlords**, but in each case he soon quarrelled with his backers and was thrown out of power.

A troubled land

During the 1920s, poverty and desolation spread across the land. The reformers who had sought to free China from imperial rule seemed rather to have destroyed it. Yet such appearances were deceptive. People who had studied the past knew that periods of trouble often occurred when long-established dynasties collapsed. They had almost always proved to be merely the lead-in to the coming of a new, more vigorous system. Most educated Chinese expected the same to happen again. The question was, with the emperors gone, where was a new political system to be found?

Rise, Brothers!

At the 4 May demonstration against the Japanese in 1919, student leaders offered a ringing call to their countrymen that ended in this way: 'We earnestly hope that all agricultural, industrial, commercial, and other groups across the entire nation will call citizens' meetings to guard our sovereignty in foreign affairs and to get rid of the traitors at home. This is the last chance for China in her life and death struggle.

'Today we swear two solemn oaths with all our fellow-countrymen: (1) that China's territory may be conquered, but it cannot be given away; and (2) that the Chinese people may be massacred, but they will not surrender.

'Our country is about to be annihilated. Rise, brothers!'

Nationalists and Communists

In the chaos after the Qing dynasty collapsed, two conflicting political forces competed to reunite the country. One was the **Guomindang**, (also spelt Kuomintang) the **Nationalist** party Sun Zhongshan had established in 1912. The other was a new arrival, the Chinese **Communist** Party (CCP).

The CCP grew out of the 4th May Movement, which provided its first leaders. Mostly students and academics, they looked for inspiration to Russia, where Lenin's **Bolsheviks** had seized power in 1917, setting up the world's first Communist government. The Chinese Communists hoped to copy the Russians, but when they held their first congress in 1921, disappointingly, only 13 delegates attended.

A common cause

As the Communist movement gathered momentum, the question of relations with the Nationalists became crucial. At first the two groups were happy to work together, since both bitterly opposed foreign interference in China, both sought an end to **warlord** power, and both wanted to reunite the nation. As long as Sun remained in charge of the Nationalists, they also shared concerns about the poverty and bad living conditions in the country.

Jiang Jieshi, shown here in 1930 when he became leader of China's Nationalist Party. He was the most powerful man in the country from 1930 until the Communist takeover in 1949.

As a result, the two parties co-operated closely for a time, with the Communists as very much the junior partners. By 1926, when the Nationalists had 200,000 members, the Communists only had 10,000. There were many people in the Nationalist movement, however, who were less than happy with the alliance. Businessmen were unhappy about the Communist-encouraged wave of strikes that spread through the cities, while landlords feared the threat of peasant unrest. As the 1920s advanced, the left and right wings of the Nationalist movement became increasingly divided.

Jiang Jieshi

In the Guomindang, as in the whole country, the matter was eventually settled by the military. The 1924 Congress had decided that the party needed its own army if it was ever to confront the warlords, and had set up a military academy to train officers to lead the force. At Sun's behest, the academy's first commander was a rising young military man named Jiang Jieshi (also spelt Chiang Kai-Shek). Jiang quickly established a reputation as an effective leader – so much so that when Sun died of liver cancer in 1925, Jiang was soon accepted as the party's new head.

The Northern Expedition

To secure his position, Jiang decided to move against the warlords who by now had much of China in their grip. From his base in Guangzhou, he launched a drive north aimed at reuniting the country under Nationalist control. This **Northern Expedition**, as it became known, was an immediate success. The well-motivated troops of Jiang's National Revolutionary Army (NRA) were able to overcome the warlords' undisciplined troops. Within a year, Jiang had all of southeastern China under his control.

The Shanghai Purge

At first the Communists, too, welcomed Jiang's success. When the NRA reached Shanghai in April 1927, they greeted the incoming troops as liberators. They were to be sadly deceived, however, for Jiang – unlike Sun – saw the Communists not as allies, but as deadly enemies. Now, without warning, he unleashed his troops on them. In the bloodbath that followed, anyone suspected of Communist sympathies was killed. In all several thousand people died.

NRA soldiers stop and search a suspected Communist during the Shanghai Purge in 1927.

The **Shanghai Purge** marked the end of any cooperation between Nationalists and Communists. From that time on, the two were deadly rivals, locked in a life-and-death struggle for the future of China. There would be 22 years of conflict before one side finally won.

Japan invades

After the **Shanghai Purge**, Jiang moved to crush the **Communist** Party once and for all. A Communist-inspired uprising in Guangdong was quickly put down, while in Wuhan as many as 100,000 people were killed for supporting Communist ideas in a massacre that lasted for months. By 1928, most members of the CCP had been driven out of the cities and forced to take refuge in the countryside. Its few remaining military forces continued some attacks from remote rural bases.

Jiang's triumph

Meanwhile the **Northern Expedition** went on. Jiang managed to win control over almost all of eastern China, where the bulk of the population lived. By the end of 1928, Beijing had been taken, and the country was reunited, at least in name. Jiang himself had been installed as chairman of a national government based in the central city of Nanjing. At a conference organized by Jiang in January 1929, the principal remaining warlords agreed to trim their armies and cut down military spending. A new mood of optimism was spreading.

However, things soon took another turn for the worse. The economic situation in China, which had been improving, started to fail again, as in the rest of the world, with the onset of the **Great Depression** of the 1930s. The warlords took this opportunity to try and regain power, and over the next four years fighting broke out many times. One confrontation in 1930 claimed almost 250,000 lives. And Jiang's city-based government did little to improve the lives of the peasants, who were still treated very badly by their landlords and suffered from bad weather conditions. A drought in 1929-30 caused a famine that killed six million people.

An English-language newspaper published in Peiping (Beijing) records the takeover of parts of Manchuria by the Japanese army in October 1931. Japan later occupied much of northern and eastern China.

The Leader EXTRA — Peiping, Sunday, October 11, 1931.

SITUATION GETTING MORE SERIOUS

JAPANESE WARSHIPS IN CHINA

LEAGUE COUNCIL CALLED TOGETHER OCTOBER 13; U. S. ALSO APPREHENSIVE

JAPAN PLANS MANCHURIAN GOVERNMENT

JAPAN'S WARNING TO CHINA

JAPAN MARINES IN NANKING; PLANES INSIDE GREAT WALL

Trouble in Manchuria

Then in 1931 fresh trouble came from an unexpected place. While the Western powers had been pulling out of China, the Japanese had maintained their trading interests in the country's three northeastern provinces, a region known outside China as **Manchuria**. Although the government in Tokyo continued friendly relations with Jiang, there were people in Japan eager to expand their control in Manchuria.

An army plot

In September 1931 the Japanese army plotters struck. Without the knowledge or approval of the Tokyo authorities, they faked an attack on a Japanese-owned railway in Manchuria, and then used the incident as an excuse to seize the capital of Manchuria, Mukden, and other cities. Against its will, the Japanese government reluctantly gave its support to the army **coup**. By 1932 Japanese forces controlled all of Manchuria, where they set up the **puppet state** of **Manchukuo**, naming China's deposed last emperor, Pu-yi, as its head of state. In the following year they extended their control to a fourth Chinese province, Jehol.

In face of this takeover of Chinese territory, Jiang did little. As a military man he knew that his own forces were no match for the powerful Japanese military machine and he still had his work cut out confronting his enemies in the rest of the country. 'The Japanese are a disease of the skin,' he would later claim, 'the Communists a disease of the heart'. It was an unpopular view with patriotic Chinese, and in the long run cost him public support.

After they renamed Manchuria as Manchukuo, the Japanese set up China's deposed last emperor, Pu-yi – shown here with his wife – as its head of state. He was a ruler in name only, and was expected to take his orders from Japan.

The Long March

After the disasters that had struck them following the **Shanghai Purge** of 1927, China's **Communists** found themselves very much on the defensive. A few organizers survived secretly in the cities, notably Shanghai. These activists tended to be very much under the influence of advisers sent from Moscow by the **Soviet** leader, Josef Stalin.

Outlaws in the hills

Other Communists had headed for the hills, living as outlaws in the countryside. By 1931 the largest of the **guerrilla** bands was based in Jiangxi province and was led by a 36-year-old named Mao Zedong. The son of a wealthy peasant, Mao was a poet and a pamphlet writer, who was also familiar with conditions in the countryside, where he had grown up. Unlike the Communists in the cities, Mao believed in the possibility of a revolution based on the peasants, not on the industrial workers, as in Russia.

Mao's Jiangxi soviet – the name given to the Communist-controlled bases – became a thorn in the flesh of Jiang Jieshi, who launched five successive 'annihilation campaigns' to destroy it. Mao effectively countered the first four attacks, but the fifth, launched in 1933, was a different matter. **Nationalist** forces surrounded the Jiangxi base, aiming to starve the rebels out. At the same time Mao's own position within the soviet was weakened by the arrival of Russian-dominated CCP leaders from Shanghai, who tried to take control.

The Long March took China's main surviving Communist force from its south-eastern base, where it was under siege from Nationalists, to a new base in Shaanxi province around the town of Yan'an. The march took 12 months and covered 10,000 kilometres.

A fighting retreat

At first the Jiangxi Communists tried to sit out the siege, but a series of military setbacks, combined with growing shortages of essential supplies, eventually forced them to plan a breakout. The main problem was where to go. The only solution seemed to be a fighting retreat, aimed to end up at one of the other, smaller soviets in a distant part of China.

The result was the **Long March**, a 10,000-kilometre odyssey that took the Communist forces west and then north across some of the harshest terrain in the country. On the way the marchers had to fight literally dozens of battles. They were also forced to cross high mountain ranges where the lightly-clad troops risked freezing to death, and marshes in which men sometimes had to sleep sitting back to back because there was not enough dry land on which to stretch out.

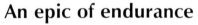

A speaker addresses a crowd of Red Army soldiers in the Yan'an base area in 1938. The Communist leader, Mao Zedong, set out to run the enclave on purely socialist lines.

An epic of endurance

Despite all the hardships, the marchers pulled through. Twelve months after they had set out, a remnant of 20,000 troops arrived at another soviet in the northern province of Shaanxi, not far from the Great Wall. They had lost more than three-quarters of the 85,000 men – there were also a few dozen women – who had started out, but they had survived as a fighting force and had been hardened and disciplined by the suffering they had experienced along the way. The leadership question had also been solved, for in the course of the trek Mao had decisively reimposed his authority. Anyone who saw the tired column straggling into their new base in October 1935, would have thought the march looked like a defeat. In fact, it proved to be the making of Mao's Communist Party.

Keeping our two feet going

Two months after the end of the Long March, Mao summed up what the survivors had endured: *'For 12 months we were under daily reconnaissance and bombing from the air by scores of aeroplanes; we were encircled, pursued, obstructed and intercepted on the ground by a force of several hundred thousand men; we encountered untold difficulties and great obstacles, but by keeping our two feet going we swept across a distance of more than 10,000 kilometres… Has there ever been a Long March like ours?'*

The Japanese push south

Even after the **Long March** ended, Jiang continued to focus his energies on fighting the **Communists** rather than the Japanese. That changed in December 1936, after an incident in Xian, the capital of Shaanxi province. Having gone there to organize yet another drive against Mao, Jiang was detained by a local **warlord**, who refused to free him unless he agreed to unite with the Communists against the invaders. At the warlord's invitation, Mao sent his right-hand man, a cultivated intellectual named Zhou Enlai, to discuss Jiang's fate. Although many Communists wished to see Jiang dead, the Russian leader Stalin sent word that he should be spared as the only leader capable of uniting China against the Japanese. So an unlikely alliance was patched up between Jiang and Mao. The two bitter foes agreed to put aside their differences in order to fight against a common enemy.

News of the Nationalist–Communist alliance caused alarm in the Japanese capital, Tokyo, where a fierce debate split the military who were by then running the country. One faction wanted to strike north from **Manchukuo** to attack the USSR, while another group wanted to drive south through China to open a pathway to southeast Asia, whose rich reserves of oil and rubber were needed by Japan to keep her own industries going. The news of Jiang and Mao's united front tipped the scales in favour of those who wanted to go south.

*On 28 July 1937 Japanese troops enter the old imperial capital of Beijing. From its base in **Manchuria** the Japanese army swept south that summer, capturing the central Chinese heartland by the end of the year.*

Invasion

In July 1937, Japanese troops clashed with Chinese soldiers guarding the Lugou Bridge, near Beijing. The Tokyo government used the incident as the pretext for a full-scale invasion, sending troops pouring south into China's eastern heartland. Beijing fell that month, and by late in the year Japanese forces had also captured Shanghai and were bombing Nanjing, the **Nationalist** capital. Jiang withdrew to the west, abandoning Nanjing to the invaders. Seeking a short war, Japan's generals spread the word to the occupying forces to make an example of the Nationalist capital. The result was an orgy of rape and killing. Foreign observers watched in horror as the Japanese troops went on the rampage against the undefended civilian population.

The Chinese retreat

If the intention of the invaders was to break Chinese morale, the plan backfired. News of the 'Rape of Nanjing', as the assault became known, only stiffened national resistance. In mid-1938, Jiang managed to temporarily delay the Japanese advance by the extreme measure of causing the Yellow River to flood its banks by breaking its dykes. Many thousands of Chinese peasants drowned or starved as a result. Within three months, however, the Japanese invaders were on the move once more, because the poorly trained and badly equipped Chinese forces were simply no match for them.

By the end of the year, almost all of China's major cities were in Japanese hands, and Jiang had been forced westward once more, establishing a new capital at Chongqing, over the mountains in remote Sichuan province. The bright future heralded by the success of the **Northern Expedition** 10 years earlier seemed to have gone for good.

A district of Shanghai lies in ruins after Japanese bombing of the city, which fell to the invaders in 1937. The Chinese military had no answer to the Japanese air force's control of the skies.

War crimes in Nanjing

At the end of World War II, an international military tribunal passed sentence on Japanese officers held responsible for war crimes committed in Nanjing. In its judgement the tribunal declared: *'In these six or seven weeks [following the capture of the city], thousands of women were raped, over 100,000 people were killed, and innumerable properties were looted and burned.'* In the case of one senior officer it judged: *'The killing of civilians was a demonstration of military prowess, and this prowess was tested by means of a competition. Nothing ever could have been more cruel and vicious, and nothing has been more barbarous.'*

Waiting out the war

By the time that World War II broke out in Europe in 1939, China was in effect divided into three unequal sections. The largest and most prosperous, in the north and east of the country, was effectively under Japanese control, although, from 1940 on, it was nominally governed by a **puppet** Chinese regime.

In the northwest, Mao's **Communists** steadily gained ground. They won support by respecting the property of the local peasants and by campaigning to reduce rents and taxes in the area they controlled. Their corner of China was poverty-stricken, so they preached economic self-reliance, encouraging small-scale industry and setting soldiers to work in the fields. Administratively they set up a system of grass-roots democracy, based on elected people's councils.

Fighting back

Yet the main reason for the Communists' increasing popularity was the **guerrilla war** they waged against the Japanese. Hitting behind enemy lines, they mobilized the peasants, sabotaged railway lines and staged surprise attacks on isolated outposts. Japanese troops responded with a campaign of reprisals summed up as the 'Three Alls' – burn all, loot all, kill all. Its savagery only drove more volunteers into the Communist camp.

Things were very different in Sichuan, where Jiang had his headquarters. Although the **Nationalists** mobilized as many as 14 million soldiers in the course of the war, their troops were mostly in poor condition and badly armed. Jiang himself once shocked a visiting American general by insisting that the Nationalist troops should only be used against Japanese forces if they outnumbered them by at least five to one.

Downriver gangsters

All too aware of his troops' limitations, Jiang chose after 1938 to play a waiting game. Convinced that Japan's drive for conquest would eventually bring it into

An American propaganda poster asks for aid for China after the USA entered the war against Japan in December 1941. US victories in the Pacific eventually forced the Japanese to pull their forces out of China in 1945.

CHINA / FIRST TO FIGHT!

MARTHA SAWYERS

UNITED CHINA RELIEF
PARTICIPATING IN NATIONAL WAR FUND

conflict with the United States, he determined to sit out the war at his Sichuan headquarters at Chongqing, conserving the bulk of his forces until American arms and money could wear Japan down. Yet even though his analysis of the situation proved correct, this wait-and-see strategy turned out to have a disastrous effect on Nationalist morale. Corruption spread as his chief supporters sought to maintain their own standard of living at the expense of the Sichuanese people. Deprived of revenues by the Japanese conquest of the cities, Jiang responded by printing large amounts of paper money. This caused massive **inflation** – prices rose 250 times between 1942 and 1944. Meanwhile local governors appointed by Jiang imposed harsh taxes on the local population, while his secret police clamped down on any protests. The Nationalist leadership became very unpopular. Behind their backs, people called them 'downriver gangsters'.

China's Communist leader Mao Zedong addresses supporters in the Yan'an base area in 1939. The son of a wealthy peasant, Mao had won unchallenged control over the movement five years earlier in the course of the **Long March**.

Maintaining an iron discipline

Mao believed from the start that the Communists could only win power if they maintained tight discipline. Early in the War of Resistance against Japan, Mao spelled out the strict rules enforced on members of the Communist Party:

'We must affirm anew the discipline of the party, namely:
1 The individual is subordinate to the organization
2 The minority is subordinate to the majority
3 The lower level is subordinate to the higher level, and
4 The entire membership is subordinate to the Central Committee.
Whoever violates these articles of discipline disrupts Party unity.'

In all, the struggle the Chinese call the War of Resistance against Japan lasted for eight years, and when the Japanese finally pulled out in 1945, it was less in response to events in China than to American victories against its troops in the Pacific battles of World War II. Even so, the long conflict cost the Chinese an estimated 1.3 million soldiers, along with an incalculable number of civilian lives. The exhausted nation wanted peace, but it was not to find it. The simmering conflict between Nationalists and Communists was once more waiting to break out, this time more bitterly than ever.

The Nationalist collapse

To an outside observer at the war's end, Jiang's **Nationalists** would have looked the favourites to provide the future government of China, with the chances of a **Communist** victory seeming slim. With the Japanese withdrawal, the Nationalists again controlled Nanjing and all the other major cities. They had more than three million soldiers under arms, while 1000 planes provided by the US Air Force gave them control of the air. Jiang had the support not just of the US government and of Britain, but also, nominally at least, of the **USSR**.

During the war between Nationalists and Communists for control of China following the Japanese withdrawal in 1945, Mao retreats on horseback from a Nationalist advance. At first the Nationalists held the upper hand in the fighting, but the tide quickly turned against them.

Civil war breaks out

At first events seemed to confirm Jiang's position. An attempt by US diplomats to restore the wartime truce between the Nationalists and Communists soon failed, and civil war once more erupted between the two groups. In the early fighting Jiang's armoured divisions were successful against the lightly-armed Communist forces, which were outnumbered by more than three to one. The Communists were even driven from their capital since the **Long March**, Yan'an. By mid-1947 the Nationalists controlled every provincial capital in China.

Collapsing morale

In 1947 the US consul in Shanghai reported back to the State Department in Washington on the state of Jiang's Nationalist troops:

'Wretched morale, mistreatment of recruits and attempted desertions are commonly reported. When marching through Shanghai recruits have to be roped together. There have been repeated incidents (two well-confirmed) where groups brought here attempted escape and were machine-gunned by guards with resultant killings.'

The curse of corruption

Beneath the surface, though, things were going badly wrong. All the problems that had plagued Jiang's government in Chongqing now resurfaced on a national scale. Corruption was rife. Chosen for their loyalty more than for their ability, many of Jiang's top officials devoted more energy to making money for themselves than to serving the people. Although Jiang still claimed to believe in democracy, his regime was authoritarian. Its repression of free speech alienated the middle classes and stirred up student protests.

Soaring prices

Worst of all, the **inflation** that had already started in the war years now spiralled out of control. By mid-1948, the asking price for 500 grams of rice had risen to a quarter of a million Chinese dollars. People's savings were used up, and those on fixed incomes, including Jiang's own troops, found their salaries were worthless even before they were paid. Morale plummeted.

The Communists were hardly affected by the inflation, as their policy of self-sufficiency meant they had little need for cash. The result was desertions from the Nationalists to the Communists on a huge scale. As early as 1947, one whole Nationalist division went over to Mao's People's Liberation Army (PLA). Then Mao's military commander, Lin Biao, launched an offensive in the north that cut off some of Jiang's best troops. Throughout 1948, defections multiplied as Nationalist soldiers happily turned their arms over to the enemy in return for a square meal; three quarters of all those who surrendered to the PLA did so without military defeat.

A Russian poster celebrates the final victory of Mao's forces in China in 1949. As the world's leading Communist power, the Soviet Union welcomed the arrival of a new recruit to the Communist camp.

Retreat to Taiwan

Mao's army captured Beijing in January 1949 and Nanjing fell three months later. Jiang was driven back to his old stronghold of Chongqing. When that in turn was threatened, he and his supporters abandoned the mainland for the island of **Taiwan** in the East China Sea, where Jiang proclaimed the **Republic** of China and set up a government in exile, vowing to return when the opportunity arose.

The People's Republic

Meanwhile on 1 October 1949 in Beijing, Mao had pronounced the foundation of the People's Republic of China. Speaking from the Gate of Heavenly Peace where new dynasties had been proclaimed in imperial times, he declared: 'Ours will no longer be a nation subject to insult and humiliation. We have stood up.' Against all the odds, Communist China had been born.

Mao takes control

The retreat of the **Nationalists** to **Taiwan** left mainland China united for the first time in more than a century. Most Chinese viewed the end of fighting and the economic stabilization that followed Mao's takeover with relief.

Mao quickly took steps to consolidate his power across the nation. One army was sent to suppress resistance in the Nationalists' southern stronghold of Guangzhou, and another to Muslim Xinjiang in the far west. A third invaded Tibet, forcibly imposing **Communist** rule on the region's Buddhist people. For the authorities in Beijing, Tibet was the Chinese province of Xizang, a part of the nation that had been temporarily separated in the time of China's weakness. For the Tibetans, however, the invasion was the start of a long and bitterly-resented foreign occupation.

Sharing out the land

Land reform was another early priority. The measures the Communists had pioneered in Yan'an were now applied across the whole country.

Land was taken away from absentee landowners and was given instead to poor peasants. The former landlords, who for centuries had ruled the countryside, were now subjected to ridicule and humiliation at 'Speak Bitterness' meetings. Many were killed in settlings of accounts by their former tenants. Some estimates put the number who died in the first few years of Communist rule as high as one million.

In the cities, the new rulers took banks, transport, gas and electricity services into public ownership. The 'Three Antis' campaign, anti-corruption, anti-waste and anti-inefficiency, was launched in 1951 to improve public services, joined the following year by the 'Five Antis' campaign, directed at business. This time the targets were bribery, fraud, tax evasion, economic sabotage and theft of state property. War was declared on gangsterism, leading to the rounding up of 130,000 'bandits and criminals' in Guangzhou

Demonstrators celebrate the revolution by burning property documents in Shanghai in 1951. One of the new regime's first acts was to transfer ownership of the land from landlords to the peasants who actually worked on it.

alone, with over half of them executed. Prostitution, gambling and drug trafficking were stamped out.

A tightening grip

The Communist Party also moved to tighten its grip on the nation's political life. All parties that would not accept Communist leadership were abolished, and the media was brought under government control.

Churches were closed and foreign missionaries expelled. Intellectuals were expected to support the new regime. Those suspected of opposing its aims were subjected to relentless 're-education' sessions in which they were repeatedly criticized, humiliated and forced to take back their former views. In the West, the term 'brainwashing' was coined to describe this process.

War in Korea

As if this radical transformation of the nation was not dramatic enough in its own right, it happened against a background of foreign war. When fighting broke out in neighbouring Korea between Communist and non-Communist forces, Mao naturally took the Communist side. He watched anxiously as a US-led United Nations force first drove the previously victorious Communists back across the **38th parallel** – the geographical line settled at World War II's end as the border between Communist and non-Communist Korea – and then pushed on almost to the Chinese border itself. Finally, in November 1951, he determined to act, sending a quarter of a million Chinese troops across the border into the battle zone.

To begin with, Mao's move was dramatically successful and the UN forces were forced to retreat back across the 38th parallel, almost into the sea. Later they rallied, and the war turned into a bloody stalemate. The cost to China was huge – nearly one million soldiers died – but Mao presented the outcome as a victory. The nation had proved that it could hold its own against a superpower. The days of foreign intrusion were well and truly over.

During the Korean War, Chinese forces break through barbed wire to clear the way for an infantry attack on enemy lines. The initial Chinese offensive was spectacularly successful. Seoul, the capital of South Korea, fell to the Communists early in 1951.

23

The fate of the 100 flowers

Since the end of World War II, the **Cold War** had divided much of the world into **capitalist** and **Communist** camps. The Korean War raised the temperature of the conflict. China and the **USSR** – the leader of the Communist bloc – had signed a friendship treaty soon after Mao came to power, and in Korea the Russians provided much military assistance for the Chinese war effort. Mao was also happy enough to follow Russian models in introducing a **Five Year Plan** for national development. The USSR had been using such plans since the 1920s to build up their economy. The first such Chinese plan, launched in 1952, not only echoed **Soviet** thinking in giving priority to heavy industry, but it was also implemented with the aid of 10,000 Russian advisers.

Peace at last

Stalin died in 1953, and soon after a truce brought the fighting in Korea to an end. Peace brought with it some prosperity for China, for the first Five Year Plan turned out to be an economic success. By the time the five years were up at the end of 1957, it had more than achieved targets and economic growth was speeding along at a rate double that of the West.

Workers operate machinery at a textile factory in Beijing soon after the Communist takeover. At first the new rulers were content to leave most heavy industry in private hands, but later control was transferred to the state.

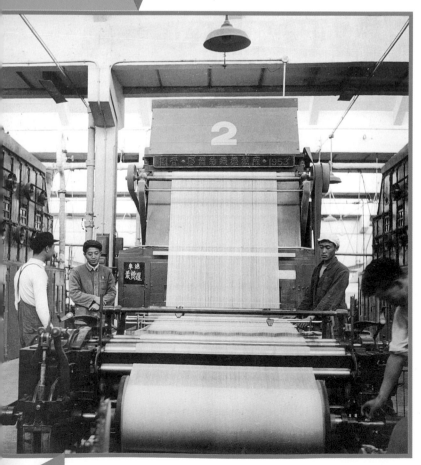

China's international prestige had also been boosted when it played a leading role in the Bandung Conference of **non-aligned** nations in 1955. But anyone who thought that success might mellow Mao was soon disappointed. Far from seeing rising affluence as a reason for loosening the ideological reins, he viewed it as a reason for more firmly imposing a Communist society. As early as 1951, he had lent his weight to a campaign to take agricultural land out of private hands and put it into common ownership. Now this policy of collectivization was driven forward faster than ever and by 1957, 96 per cent of all land was held by peasants' **co-operatives**.

By that time events in the USSR had taken a dramatic turn. In February 1956 Nikita Khrushchev, the new Soviet leader, surprisingly launched a bitter attack on his predecessor, Stalin. Among other failings, Khrushchev accused Stalin of having built a 'cult of personality' around himself at the expense of the people. Mao, whose status in China closely recalled that of the dead leader in the USSR, could not help but see the criticism as a reflection on his own position.

Soviet leader Nikita Khrushchev shakes hands with Mao on a visit to Beijing in 1954. Relations between the USSR and China were close at the time, although the friendship rapidly cooled.

'Let 100 flowers bloom'

Mao's response was unexpected. Having convinced himself that Stalin's mistake lay in having become cut off from the Russian people, he now determined to renew his own links with the Chinese. To the alarm of many in the Communist hierarchy, he called for a new openness in public debate, inviting individuals to express their true feelings about the state of China under Communist rule. Dissenting views were to be encouraged. 'Let 100 flowers bloom,' he declared, 'and let 100 schools of thought contend.'

Students speak out

At first he found few willing to speak out. Memories of the thought control movement of the preceding years were too fresh. But when Mao renewed his appeal later in the year, he began to get his wish. Hand-written posters started appearing in the streets, attacking heavy-handed bureaucracy and sometimes even attacking named Communist Party officials. The protests were most common around the nation's universities, professors and students alike, joining in the calls for reform.

By June 1957 the government's critics were gaining courage. Some posters now dared to attack the very idea of rule by one party and, by implication at least, by Mao himself. This was too much for the Chinese leader. Abruptly he put the policy into reverse. Dissent of any kind once more became a crime.

The great leap forward

The 100 Flowers experience confirmed Mao's low opinion of intellectuals, but it left his faith in China's peasants undimmed. As 1957 drew to a close, he decided to launch a new piece of political theatre intended to capitalize on the **Five Year Plan's** successes.

Scrapping blueprints for a second plan, he determined to mobilize the nation instead for a burst of communal effort that became known as the Great Leap Forward. The project was to last for just three years, not five, and it was intended to achieve huge rates of growth.

Becoming self-sufficient

To achieve these miracles, China's 600 million people were expected to do more than just work hard: they had to change their way of life. The agricultural **co-operatives** that had only just been set up were now regrouped in **communes** containing many thousands of people. Each one was encouraged to be self-sufficient, not just in food but even in essential materials like steel. The backyard steel furnace was to become the Great Leap Forward's most familiar symbol.

A propaganda poster from the time of the Great Leap Forward shows a happy worker employed at a newly opened oilfield. The slogan says: 'Rely on your own efforts to build up our motherland.'

Early hopes

In the first year of the programme, real progress was made, and many large-scale irrigation and construction projects were undertaken. On the communes, too, great advances seemed to be under way, but here appearances were deceptive. To meet quotas set in Beijing, peasants were diverted from the familiar tasks they did well to new ones – like steel-making – that they often did badly. Because Mao wanted spectacular gains in wheat and rice production, other essential crops were abandoned and fish ponds were filled in.

Even so, the 1958 harvest was a good one, though not as good as local party officials reported. Eager to please the authorities in Beijing, they also failed to pass on the many problems that the programme was encountering. As it happened, they had good reason for not speaking out. When China's Defence Minister Peng Dehuai, a veteran of the **Long March** and an old friend of Mao's, told him that all was not well, Mao responded by having him dismissed from his post. Meanwhile, Mao himself raised his expectations for the following year.

Catastrophe

At this point the notoriously unreliable Chinese climate turned against the plan. 1960 saw floods in the south of the country and drought in the north. Food production plummeted. Yet officials in Beijing, lulled by the false reports that were still reaching them, failed to realize the extent of the problem, and continued to demand large supplies of grain as taxation from districts that no longer had enough to feed their own people. This bad administration turned a natural disaster into a catastrophe, and many millions starved as a result.

Defeat for Mao

By late 1960 the extent of the tragedy was at last clear, and Mao had to accept responsibility. For him, it represented a considerable defeat and for a time he withdrew from an active part in government. For the nation as a whole, the project's failure meant not just many individual tragedies, but also the loss of much of the ground gained in the Five Year Plan. Ironically, the Great Leap Forward turned out really to have been a giant step backward for China.

A photo, staged to reassure workers of the Great Leap Forward's success, shows happy peasants celebrating a bumper harvest in 1959. In fact food shortfalls that year and the next caused a famine in which millions of people died.

An ecological disaster

One of the stranger actions of the Great Leap Forward was a campaign against sparrows, who were blamed for reducing agricultural productivity by stealing seeds. Across the nation, farm labourers were encouraged to bang pots and pans ceaselessly to keep sparrows in the air until they dropped dead from exhaustion. But the result of the operation was not what the authorities expected. With fewer birds to keep numbers down, insects multiplied to plague proportions, devastating crops and spreading disease.

Cultural revolution

After the failure of the Great Leap Forward, Mao's position was seriously weakened. He lost one of his main government positions – that of state chairman – to the less hardline Liu Shaoqi. Over the next few years the running of the country passed increasingly into the hands of Liu and his chief aide, a rising politician called Deng Xiaoping. Deng's practical views were summed up in his much-quoted saying: 'It doesn't matter if a cat is black or white so long as it catches mice.'

Changing attitudes

Brooding on his problems, Mao became convinced that they were the same as those facing the country as a whole. The revolution in people's attitudes that he had long dreamed of had not happened, and the reason could only lie in traditional Chinese culture and the respect for old ways that it promoted. An entirely new attitude was needed, he decided, if he was to create the equal society he sought.

In 1964 he set up a **Cultural Revolution** group to fight against traditional habits, but under its first chairman, the mayor of Beijing, it did little. So Mao turned instead to his own wife, Jiang Qing, a former actress, who flung herself into the task of transforming Chinese culture with enthusiasm.

A coded message

The huge upheaval that became known as the Cultural Revolution found its initial spark in the most unlikely source: a theatre review. One of Jiang's allies wrote a bitter review of a play called 'Hai Rui Dismissed from Office', whose plot concerned the sacking of an honest official by a powerful 16th-century emperor for speaking out against abuses. This, the reviewer claimed, was actually an attack on Mao, intended to remind people of his sacking of Peng Dehuai for pointing out the failures of the Great Leap Forward.

The Red Guards

In the course of the controversy stirred up by the review, Mao took the side of

*Students write anti-capitalist slogans on posters in 1967, near the start of the Cultural Revolution. Inspired by Mao, the movement aimed to destroy all ways of thinking and behaving that clashed with the **Communist** Party ideas.*

those who were critical of the play, speaking out against what he called a 'Beijing Black Gang' of bureaucrats seeking to undermine the revolution. Students took Mao's lead, and posters attacking Liu Shaoqi's administration appeared around Beijing. At the university, some students started calling themselves **Red Guards**, dedicated to preserving the revolution. Mao engineered the demotion of his chief rivals at a party convention, then attended a mass student rally wearing a Red Guard armband.

Attacking the 'Four Olds'

His backing unleashed a flood of revolutionarily-minded youth across the country. At his suggestion, Red Guards were allowed to travel free on the state-run railways and were given lodgings at their destinations. All over the country they went on the rampage, destroying anything representative of the 'Four Olds' – old culture, old ideas, old customs and old habits. People associated with the old ways were targeted. Subjected to public humiliation, they were forced to confess their supposed wrong-doing. Many were beaten up or killed.

Among the chief victims were Mao's political enemies. Liu Shaoqi died naked in a concrete cell. His wife, accused of Western decadence, was paraded before thousands of people in a slit-skirt evening dress and a necklace of ping-pong balls, mocking her supposed love of pearls. Chen Yi, China's Foreign Minister, was exhibited in a dunce's cap.

During the Cultural Revolution, schoolgirls read aloud from the 'Little Red Book' that contained the thoughts of Chairman Mao, seen waving on a giant poster in the background.

Spreading chaos

By mid-1967 the violence was increasing. A confrontation between Red Guards and angry workers and soldiers in the city of Wuhan turned into open fighting. A People's **Commune** briefly took over in Shanghai, and in Beijing foreign embassies were attacked, as in the days of the **Boxer Rebellion**. Mao decided to call a halt.

Two more years passed before the forces of the Cultural Revolution were brought fully under control. By that time, Mao's last great drive to radicalize China had brought the country close to civil war and left many thousands dead.

China and the Cold War

Throughout the **Cultural Revolution,** China continued to play a part in the international politics of the **Cold War**, though in an unexpected way. At a time when Mao was stressing revolutionary purity in China, his foreign policy moved from alliance with the fellow-Communist **USSR** to a bitter hostility. This led China eventually to forge ties with its former Enemy Number One, the USA.

Falling out with the Soviets

The reasons for the falling-out were partly personality clashes, partly ideological differences, and partly rivalry over who should lead the **Communist** world. The differences first emerged at the time of the Great Leap Forward, which the **Soviet** leader Nikita Khrushchev publicly ridiculed. In 1960 the split came into the open when Khrushchev abruptly stopped military and economic aid to China and ordered all Russian advisers to leave the country.

Over the next few years the war of words between the Communist powers grew steadily louder. Both sides claimed that the other had moved away from the path of true Communism. Relations reached a low point in 1962 when China became involved in a border dispute with India that flared into a month-long war. The USSR said publicly that it was neutral, but privately supplied the Indian military with MiG fighter planes. The Chinese bitterly criticized their former allies for what they saw as treachery.

Russian soldiers patrol the Soviet-Chinese border in March 1969, when the two Communist powers – once friends – came close to war after clashes along the Ussuri River frontier.

Mao on nuclear war

In 1958 Mao made a speech to a Communist Party Congress that particularly worried the Russians, helping persuade Soviet Premier Nikita Khrushchev that he was dangerously irresponsible. *'We have no experience of atomic war,'* Mao claimed. *'We do not know how many people would die. It would be better if half the population were left; next best would be a third. ... After several more* **Five Year Plans***, China would rise up again.* **Capitalism** *would be destroyed, and in its place we would have perpetual peace. That would be no bad thing.'*

China's atom bomb

For the next 10 years the split between the Soviets and Chinese divided the Communist world. For China, one result of this split was that the nation was forced to make its own way in scientific research. Mao took all the more pride in the development in 1964 of the first Chinese atomic bomb, followed three years later by a hydrogen bomb. Meanwhile relationships with the Soviets continued to get worse, reaching an all-time low in 1969 when fighting broke out briefly between the two powers along their 7000-kilometre joint border.

My enemy's enemy

The USA watched the split with satisfaction. Regarding the Soviets as their main enemy, American government officials tried to establish links with China on the principle that 'My enemy's enemy is my friend.' A first step was made in 1969, when some restrictions on US trade with China were lifted.

Serious obstacles remained in the path of improved relations, however. The most difficult was the US's backing for Jiang Jieshi's **Nationalist** regime on **Taiwan**, which the Americans considered the official government of China. It seemed therefore a major change in US policy when, in 1971, US President Richard Nixon finally agreed to admit mainland China to the United Nations **UN** in place of Taiwan. For the Chinese, the switch was an important victory, and a triumph for the subtle diplomacy of Mao's long-serving **henchman**, Zhou Enlai.

US President Richard Nixon takes time off from diplomacy to go sightseeing on the Great Wall during his groundbreaking visit to China in 1972. The trip signalled the beginning of a warming of relations between the two countries.

Warmer relations

The change in US policy at the UN paved the way for a rapid warming in relations between the two countries. The new relationship was cemented in 1972 when President Richard Nixon agreed to make a state visit to Beijing. Although still suspicious of each other, Chinese and American leaders were prepared from then at least to co-operate with one another. This was a great change for two nations that had confronted each other on the battlefield 20 years earlier in the Korean War.

The end of Mao

The **Cultural Revolution** officially came to an end in 1969 with the gathering of the Ninth Congress of the **Communist** Party. It left China in tatters, with its educational system and industry at a standstill, and gangs of lawless youths roaming the city streets. The first task was to restore law and order, and this was mainly done by the army. Young people were encouraged to go to the countryside to learn from the peasants, and many millions took up this challenge. The threat in the cities was defused.

The fall of Lin Biao

One of the few people to have gained from the chaos of the Cultural Revolution was China's Defence Minister, Lin Biao, a hero of the civil war. Lin was believed to be Mao's choice to eventually succeed him, but this was a dangerous position to hold since Mao was very suspicious of rivals for power. As events turned out, Lin was dead within two years, killed with his family in a mysterious plane crash in Mongolia. There were rumours that he had tried to stage a **coup** against Mao, and when it failed had tried to leave the country. Whether his plane simply ran out of fuel or was shot down has never been established.

The Gang of Four

Lin's death and the new relationship with the USA opened the way for Zhou Enlai to return to centre stage. He set about repairing the damage done by the Cultural Revolution, surrounding himself with other moderates, including Liu Shaoqi's old **henchman** Deng Xiaoping. But the **pragmatists** did not have the field to themselves. Mao's wife, Jiang Qing, remained politically powerful, even though she and Mao had by now separated. With three hard-left allies, she formed a group known to its enemies as the **Gang of Four**, whose principal goal was to keep the spirit of the Cultural Revolution alive.

Divide and rule

Now weakened by Parkinson's disease, Mao himself took little direct part in politics after the 1972 meeting with President Nixon. He was content to follow a policy of 'Divide and rule', leaving the left- and right-wing factions to fight it out for his support.

Matters came to a head in 1976, a critical year for modern China. In January, Zhou Enlai died, depriving the moderates of their figurehead. His death caused an outpouring of grief across the nation that quickly took on a political dimension. The Gang of Four tried to stifle any public demonstrations of mourning and ordered the removal of wreaths laid in Zhou's honour at Beijing's Monument of the Heroes. When word of this action got around, crowds of protesters hurried to the scene, only to be brutally dispersed by the police. The Gang of Four's supporters accused Deng of having organized the show of strength, and managed to have him dismissed from his official positions.

Mao dies

Then on 9 September Mao himself died. China had lost its 'Great Helmsman', the man who had unified the nation and steered it through its revolution. In shock at his death, the whole nation mourned.

Mao's place in history remains controversial, although no one would deny his central importance. On the plus side, his dedication to improving the fortunes of the mass of the Chinese people was sincere and unwavering, and he left the country infinitely stronger than he found it. The downside included his changeable approach to policy-making, his capacity for hatred, and his total inability to tolerate opposition. In his last years, he compared himself with China's first emperor, and in the long run of Chinese history, it is with the founders of imperial dynasties that he may be compared: eccentric, tyrannical, sometimes bloodthirsty, but undoubtedly effective in changing the course of the nation.

Following Mao's death in September 1976, a million people attended this memorial gathering in Beijing's Tiananmen Square, honouring the man who had led the country for the past quarter-century.

Deng the survivor

Mao's death unleashed a power struggle that set the far-left faction of his widow Jiang Qing and her allies against more moderate elements in the party. It was quickly over because Jiang did not have enough support in the ranks of the **Communist** Party or in the army to mount an effective challenge. The **Gang of Four** were arrested and imprisoned.

A need for change

Mao's immediate successor was a Communist Party loyalist called Hua Guofeng, whose policy was summed up by critics as the 'Two Whatevers': whatever Mao said was right, whatever Mao did must be continued. But the mood of the country demanded change. Within three years, Hua had been ousted by the veteran Deng Xiaoping, now 74 years old. Although he refused to take a an official government position, Deng was given the title 'paramount leader', and it soon became evident that he was setting the nation's course.

For Deng, this success was even more amazing considering the reversals he had known in his career. He had twice held high office, under Liu Shaoqi and Zhou Enlai, but each time he had been forced out by the hard left. In the **Cultural Revolution** his life had been at risk. Although he had survived by living quietly in the provinces, his son had been attacked by **Red Guards** and left paralyzed from the waist down.

The trial of the Gang of Four

Mao's widow, Jiang Qing, and her three political associates were finally put on trial in 1980, four years after their arrest. The charges against them were sometimes bizarre. Besides being held responsible for the deaths of many thousands of people in the Cultural Revolution, Jiang Qing was also accused of such minor infractions as eating golden carp (an expensive luxury), taking out library books about past empresses, playing poker while Mao lay dying, and watching foreign videos, particularly *The Sound of Music*. She was found guilty and sentenced to death, later reduced to life imprisonment. She died in prison in 1991.

*Deng Xiaoping, photographed at the age of 74. A comrade-in-arms of Mao during the **Long March**, he twice fell from favour, but each time bounced back to a leadership position in the Communist Party.*

The Four Modernizations

Now Deng's reputation as a cautious reformer came to his aid. The nation was tired of political drama and what it wanted was to move down the path of economic development. Deng had been Zhou's principal assistant in drawing up a reform programme that became known as the Four Modernizations – of industry, defence, technology and education. Seeking to continue on that path, the party looked to

him to improve living standards while keeping the Communist Party as the only party of government.

Women employees in a Shanghai factory work to boost industrial efficiency. Under Deng's reforms, workers who produced more could earn higher wages than those who produced less.

Profits from the land

Deng's first priority was agriculture, which still employed 80 per cent of the population. The **communes** set up at the time of the Great Leap Forward were dropped and although land remained the property of the state, the focus of production now became the village, and within it the individual peasant household. Under the Responsibility System that Deng introduced, individual families were still expected to meet a grain quota set by the state, but they were to be allowed to sell any surplus at rural markets and keep the proceeds. As a result, production soared.

Perhaps the biggest innovation under Deng was a new stress on practical results rather than on ideology. Business people were now praised for their drive; 'to get rich is no sin,' Deng insisted. Party secretary Hu Yaobang even went so far as to declare publicly that Communism could not solve all China's problems. The change from the days of the Cultural Revolution could hardly have been stronger.

The half-open door

At the same time as allowing profits again in agriculture, Deng sought to revitalize industry. Where all workers had once been paid the same whether they did a good or a bad job, now there were extra wages for the most productive employees. Once jobs had been for life, but now managers were given the power to hire and fire. Prices of goods had formerly been set by the state, but now they were to be allowed to rise and fall.

The open-door Policy

Even more radically, Deng adopted an **'open-door'** policy of welcoming money and expert help from abroad. This approach marked a reversal, since in the **Cultural Revolution**, any contact with the outside world had been forbidden. Now Deng sent students off by the thousands to Western universities to study science, engineering and business studies. Foreign technology flooded into the country as part of the drive to modernize Chinese industry. To encourage outside investment, four Special Economic Zones (SEZs) were set up in the southeast of the country, where China's export industries were concentrated.

A rush to the towns

Economically, the programme proved an immediate success. One result was a rush of people to the towns. Between 1980 and 1986, the urban population grew from 200 million to 371 million – still not much more than a third of the total population, but a huge increase. New industries flourished and China became the world's largest manufacturer of washing machines and colour televisions.

Even so, the new openness operated within strict limits. Alongside the Four Modernizations, Deng also promoted what he called the Four Cardinal Principles: keeping to the socialist road, preserving the people's democratic dictatorship, maintaining leadership by the **Communist** Party and upholding **Marxism–Leninism** and the thoughts of Mao Zedong. Economic change was balanced against social conservatism.

Deng's balancing act

Yet Deng's balancing act proved a difficult one to manage. Opening up China to outside investment of money also exposed it to new ideas. Foreign firms investing in China brought in their own notions of how work should be organized. Students sent abroad to study came back hankering for the freedom of expression they had outside China.

A poster in a busy Beijing street promotes the benefits of the one-child policy, an attempt to slow China's spiralling population growth. The programme encouraged couples, under threat of fines and other penalties, to have just one baby.

Demanding democracy

The result was an upsurge in demands for what became unofficially known as the Fifth Modernization: democracy. The mood first found expression in the Democracy Wall movement of the late 1970s. Following a tradition dating back to the days of the 100 Flowers, protesters put up hand-written posters criticizing the authorities on a wall in Beijing. The government soon cracked down on the practice and in 1980 references to freedom of speech were even removed from the constitution.

But the seeds of discontent had been sown. So long as the nation was getting richer, as it was in the first years of Deng's reforms, the voices demanding change faded into the background. However, they did not go away, and when the economy took a turn for the worse, they were ready to be heard again loud and clear.

The one-child policy

China's spiralling population topped one billion shortly after Deng took control. Realizing that living standards could not improve if the number of people in the nation grew faster than its resources, he decided to take drastic measures to reduce the growth rate. From 1981, he launched a campaign to restrict families to just one child. Those who had more, except under special circumstances, were punished by fines and the withdrawal of some health and education benefits. The policy succeeded in cutting the birth rate by almost half, but was deeply unpopular in the countryside, where large families had traditionally been a guarantee of cheap labour to work the land.

Tiananmen Square

By the mid-1980s, ten years after Mao's death, problems were becoming apparent in Deng's modernization programme. Grain production had stopped rising as farmers switched to other, more profitable cash crops, and there were again fears of hunger in the countryside. In the cities, industrial productivity had soared, but jobs were less secure. Other social problems were also attracting attention. Crime was on the rise, and growing unemployment had put people on the streets. There were reckoned to be 670,000 beggars across the nation.

Campus protests

In 1986 public unhappiness with the changes surfaced in a wave of protests and demonstrations, mostly centred on university campuses. The authorities responded with a campaign against liberalism and Western influences. One of its symptoms was seen as Western fashions, and there was a crackdown on youths with long hair and young women wearing high heels or make-up. More significantly, the **Communist** Party secretary Hu Yaobang, known to be sympathetic to the demonstrators, was forced from office.

An old woman begs for money from passers-by in a Beijing street. Deng's economic reforms widened the gap between rich and poor in 1980s China.

The death of Hu

For a time the repression of the protestors worked and they were silenced, but that changed with the death of Hu in April 1989. Posters soon appeared comparing the dead man's virtues with the failings of the surviving leadership: 'A true man has died; false ones are still living,' one proclaimed. Then, as had happened following Zhou Enlai's death in 1976, demonstrators flocked to Tiananmen Square on the day of Hu's funeral to express their grief.

At first the government took no action, even though such demonstrations had been declared illegal. Then students set up a makeshift camp in the square and announced that they were going on hunger strike in demand of democratic reform.

For almost a month the protesters retained control of Tiananmen Square, China's ceremonial heart, while the government argued over how to respond to the situation. Hardliners, led by Deng, wanted to send in the army, but they were fiercely opposed by moderates desperate to find a peaceful solution. Eventually the hardliners prevailed, but even then the army proved reluctant to act. Thousands of Beijing citizens blocked their path, and the troops had no orders to shoot their way through.

The hardliners win

Meanwhile the students in the square were becoming more outspoken in their demands. They erected a 10-metre-high replica of the Statue of Liberty, openly proclaiming their sympathy for Western ideas of democracy. Two more weeks of government argument passed before the hardliners finally won the day. On the night of 23 June 1989, armoured troop carriers moved in on the square, and this time the soldiers had orders to fire. There was some fighting. One troop carrier was crippled by a firebomb and a crew member who escaped from the flames was lynched. Other troops started shooting at the crowd. By dawn the following morning, the students had been moved out and the square stood empty.

Student protesters crowd Tiananmen Square in central Beijing at the height of the pro-democracy demonstrations in June 1989. Soon afterwards, Red Army troops moved in and cleared the square at the cost of many lives.

A hollow victory

In all, the fighting in Tiananmen Square and elsewhere in Beijing accounted for several hundred civilian lives, and more were lost in similar showdowns in other major cities. There was never any doubt who would win, as the students could not hope to match the firepower of the People's Liberation Army. So, 13 years after he himself had encouraged protests in the square in the cause of reform, the 85-year-old Deng emerged victorious from a much bloodier confrontation. But the opponents he had vanquished were the best and brightest of the younger generation – the very people that he needed to ensure the future of his modernization policies. Abroad, China stood condemned of killing its own citizens when they raised their voices for freedom.

Boom times on the coast

Although the Tiananmen Square disaster damaged China's reputation abroad and set back the campaign for democracy at home, it did not change the direction of government policy. Deng sought to explain what had happened to the Chinese people as the work of bad elements trying to destroy the nation's stability. Politically he continued to follow a policy of repression, sending anyone suspected of secret opposition to prison camps.

Opening up for trade

Above all, the economic reforms continued. By the early 1990s most of China was opened up for trade. The process was helped by American policy. Believing that the best way to encourage political progress in China was to encourage contact with the outside world, the American government gave China **'most favoured nation'** trading status in 1992.

By that time the modernization programme had helped transform life for many Chinese, at least in the nation's coastal provinces. Between 1981 and 1991, the bulk of the goods China exported multiplied five times over and the amount of foreign investment coming into the country grew four times. The country became used to annual growth rates of more than 10 per cent, among the highest in the world. Between Deng's emergence as paramount leader in 1978, and 1994 when he made his last public appearance, gross domestic product, the volume of all goods produced in the nation, increased by four times.

Accompanied by Deng's successor Jiang Zemin, US President Bill Clinton inspects troops on a state visit to China in 1998.
*Throughout the 1990s, China continued to pursue an **open-door** policy of increasing trade and educational contacts with the outside world.*

A new leader

Deng finally died at the age of 92 in 1997. His chosen successor was a technically minded man named Jiang Zemin, who had served as mayor of Shanghai in the 1980s. Jiang continued to follow Deng's economic and political policies, although he travelled abroad more than earlier leaders, seeking to project an image of a stable and modernized China. At the same time, he maintained tight political control at home.

Hong Kong returned

Five months after Deng's death, some unfinished business was completed when Hong Kong was returned to Chinese rule. Originally seized by the British after the first Opium War in 1842, Hong Kong had long been a reminder of China's 19th-century weakness. It was also a hive of industry and prosperity and a model for the Special Economic Zones created near it in the rest of China in the 1980s.

In 1898 Britain had been granted a 99-year lease on the land around Hong Kong, an area known as the New Territories. In 1984 Deng and the British prime minister of the day, Margaret Thatcher, signed an agreement for the return of the entire colony – the territories and the city itself – when the lease ran out in 1997. In return China promised to preserve Hong Kong's existing economic and social system for at least 50 years. The colony was handed back on schedule and when the nearby Portuguese enclave of Macau was given over two years later, all surviving reminders of the **unequal treaties** were finally gone. Many Chinese saw in the 'one nation, two systems' agreement over Hong Kong a blueprint for the eventual return of **Taiwan**, which still remained firmly in **Nationalist** hands as the millennium drew to a close.

High-rise blocks line the waterfront of the port city of Hong Kong, handed back to China by the British when the 99-year lease on the surrounding land ran out in 1997.

The fate of Tibet

While coastal China prospered in the 1990s, the picture remained different in the far west, where another China of poverty and embittered national minorities survived. The best known of these is Tibet, which has suffered terribly since its seizure by the Red Army in 1950. Ethnic Chinese flooded in to dilute the Tibetan population, and in the **Cultural Revolution** much of the nation's cultural heritage, including 90 per cent of its monasteries, were destroyed. Throughout the 1980s and '90s its people continued their resistance to the Chinese presence. China's attitude to Tibet seems surprising as it has always been bitterly opposed to colonialization elsewhere in the world.

21st-century China

In economic terms, China entered the 3rd millennium almost as two separate countries. One was prosperous, at least by past standards. This China was concentrated in the provinces lining the nation's 5600-kilometre coast. Inland was another China, growing progressively poorer the further it lay from the sea, a land first of rice and grain fields and then of mountains and deserts, parched in summer and freezing cold in winter, where grinding poverty was still an everyday reality.

At the crossroads

Politically, too, the nation was pulled in two directions. As the 21st century dawned, China's leaders were trying, as they had done for more than two decades, to tread a path between the two extremes – opening to the West economically, while still retaining tight political control. China was still a one-party state, it continued to imprison dissidents and its human-rights record was bad.

The new China

Even so, outside observers saw grounds for hope. China was changing in profound ways that in time, they believed, must lead to demands for a more open and democratic society. The population was not only increasingly urban, but also better educated and better nourished. The proportion of the population with at least a high school education was growing by one percent every year and average height was increasing by 2 cm every 10 years. This new, more sophisticated China would soon want not just more consumer goods, but also greater freedom of speech and an increased say in the organization of its citizens' lives – or so the optimists believed.

Neon signs light up the night sky in the entertainment district of Shanghai. The port city's economy boomed with the growth of trade in the decades following the death of Mao.

Population pressures

Not all the developments in China were positive, however. Although the one-child policy proved effective in slowing population growth, it still left the nation as easily the world's most populous, with 1.2 billion people – one in every five people on Earth. Of that total, more than a billion live on only one-sixth of the nation's land area, in the east and along the fertile river valleys, creating problems of overcrowding and pollution. The country also has the largest armed forces in the world, with more than four million men and women in service.

Farm workers use a bicycle cart to move hay in the Chinese countryside. The growing wealth of China has been lop-sided, with most going to the eastern cities and little to rural areas.

A deep desire for order

Only time can tell whether China will move peacefully to greater democracy and a closer integration with the rest of the world. Even if economic modernization does encourage political liberalization, it may not take the form that the West expects. The fact is that China has a long and proud heritage that does not include a tradition of representative democracy. Instead, the nation's history has been one in which periods of effective **authoritarian** government have alternated with times of **anarchy** and banditry. Modern China's inhabitants may want human rights, but many of them also retain a deep fear of the country falling apart once more, as it most recently did in the 1920s.

As a result, there is strong support for firm government, so long as it is seen to be even-handed and not corrupt. Any democratic movement that is to succeed in China in the future must first convince the people that it can deliver stability, prosperity and civic order as well as democratic rights.

China timeline

1900	Boxer Rebellion targets foreigners in China.
1908	Death of Empress Dowager Cixi.
1911	Revolution sweeps away China's last imperial dynasty.
1912	The Republic of China is proclaimed with Sun Zhongshan as its provisional president, soon replaced by Yuan Shikai. Nationalist Party founded, with Sun Zhongshan as its chairman.
1916	Yuan Shikai dies after trying unsuccessfully to have himself declared emperor. Start of warlord era.
1919	4 May Movement of patriotic student demonstrations.
1921	First Congress of Chinese Communist Party (CCP).
1925	Death of Sun Zhongshan.
1926	Jiang Jieshi, the Nationalists' new leader, launches the Northern Expedition against the warlords to reunite the country.
1927	Shanghai Purge: Nationalists turn on their former Communist allies.
1928	Northern Expedition reaches Beijing. Jiang heads a national government.
1930	Famine following three years of drought kills millions of Chinese.
1931	Japanese troops seize China's three north-eastern provinces.
1932	Japanese proclaim the kingdom of Manchukuo in the occupied provinces, with the last Qing emperor as its puppet ruler.
1934	Communists begin the Long March.
1935	Long March ends in northern Shaanxi province.
1936	The Xian incident: a northern warlord detains Jiang Jieshi until he agrees to unite with the Communists against the Japanese.
1937	Japanese troops invade China from Manchukuo. The Rape of Nanjing.
1945	End of World War II. Defeated, Japan withdraws from China.
1946	Civil war breaks out between Nationalists and Communists.
1948	Inflation cripples the Chinese economy.
1949	Communist troops capture Beijing and Nanjing. The People's Republic of China is established, with Mao Zedong as its leader.
1950	Red Army invades Tibet. China and USSR sign a friendship treaty. China enters the Korean War.
1952	China launches the Five Year Plan.
1957	Mao launches the '100 Flowers' campaign of free speech.
1958	Start of the Great Leap Forward.
1960	Widespread famine marks the Great Leap Forward's end. USSR withdraws all advisers from China.
1962	Liu Shaoqi and Deng Xiaoping take over day-to-day administration of the government. Border war with India.
1964	China's first atomic bomb exploded.
1966	Liu and Deng dismissed. Cultural Revolution breaks out.
1967	China's first hydrogen bomb exploded.
1969	Fighting breaks out on the Chinese-Soviet border.
1971	People's Republic of China replaces Taiwan as China's representative at the United Nations.
1972	US President Nixon visits China.
1976	Death of Zhou Enlai triggers Tiananmen Square demonstrations. Death of Mao Zedong. Gang of Four arrested.
1978	Deng Xiaoping emerges as paramount leader. Democracy Wall movement flourishes.
1984	China and Britain issue joint declaration on future of Hong Kong.
1986	A wave of protests in Chinese universities spark a crackdown on 'bourgeois liberalism'.
1989	Pro-democracy demonstrations are bloodily suppressed in Tiananmen Square.
1992	USA confers 'most favoured nation' trading status on China.
1997	Death of Deng Xiaoping. Hong Kong returned to Chinese control by Britain.

Further reading

Books: History

First Apple, by Ching Yeung Russell (Boyds Mills Press, 1994)

China's Long March, by Jean Fritz (Putnam, 1988)

The Chinese Cultural Revolution, by David Pietrusza (Gale Group, 1997)

The Long March: The Making of Modern China (Turning Points in History), by Tony Allan (Heinemann, 2001)

Country Studies: China, by Trevor Higginbottom & Tony White (Heinemann, 1999)

Books: Fiction

The Good Earth, by Pearl S Buck, (Washington Square Press, 1994)

Books: Personal accounts

Wild Swans, by Jung Chang. (Flamingo, 1993)

Red Scarf Girl: A Memoir of the Cultural Revolution, by Ji–Li Jiang (HarperCollins, 1998)

Website

www.insidechina.com

Glossary

abdicate to step down voluntarily from power

anarchy a complete breakdown of law and order; also a political system that believes there should be no government hierarchy

authoritarian an extremely strict form of government that does not allow dissent

Bolshevik follower of the Communist leader Lenin in the Russian Revolution

Boxer Rebellion popular uprising against foreign influence in China at the start of the 20th century

capitalism economic system based on private ownership of the means of production

Cold War state of hostility dividing much of the world after World War II between a capitalist bloc led by the USA and a Communist bloc led by the USSR

commune in China, a group of villages and farms pooling ownership of the land and expected to meet production targets set by the state

Communist a follower of communism, a political movement which aims to create a classless society in which the means of production are owned in common

co-operatives in China, agricultural units, generally smaller than communes, in which ownership of tractors and other machinery was shared

coup the overthrow of a government

Cultural Revolution movement launched by Mao Zedong in 1966 to change ways of thought and wipe out old customs and habits

egalitarian a belief in the equality of all people, manifested by the desire to abolish extremes of rich and poor in society

exile when a citizen is forced to leave the country

Five Year Plan s tate-directed development programmes applied in Communist countries with the aim of speeding up economic growth. China's first Five Year Plan lasted from the start of 1953 to the end of 1957

Gang of Four group of four prominent left-wing activists, led by Mao Zedong's wife Jiang Qing, who helped steer policy in the Cultural Revolution

Great Depression economic depression that caused unemployment and poverty around the world in the 1930s

guerrilla war type of warfare based on small, irregular units rather than standing armies

Guomindang the Chinese name for the Nationalist Party, originally set up by Sun Zhongshan in 1912

hardliner a person who will not admit of any change or relaxation of his party's policies

henchman a servant and loyal supporter

inflation rising prices

kowtow traditional Chinese salute involving touching the forehead to the floor

Long March fighting retreat by Communist troops under Mao Zedong in 1935-36 to escape encirclement by Nationalists

Manchuria name used outside China to describe the northeastern region of the country, made up of the three provinces of Liaoning, Jilin and Heilongjiang

Manchukuo puppet state set up in Manchuria by Japanese forces in the 1930s

Marxism-Leninism the Russian form of Communism as inspired by the writings of Marx and the political leadership of Lenin

most favoured nation status status granted to selected nations by the US government guaranteeing favourable terms of trade

Nationalists supporters of the Guomindang political party set up by Sun Zhongshan in 1912 and later run by Jiang Jieshi

non-aligned word used to describe countries not forming part of either the capitalist or Communist blocs in the Cold War

Northern Expedition military campaign conducted by Jiang Jieshi against the warlords in 1926-28

NRA national Revolutionary Army; the armed forces of the Nationalist movement

open door policy of encouraging trade links with the rest of the world pursued by Deng Xiaoping from the early 1980s onward

pragmatist a politician who bases his policies not on hard-and-fast principles but on whatever works

puppet state a government claiming to be independent that is in fact controlled by another

Red Guards in the Cultural Revolution, young agitators dedicated to achieving Mao's goals of destroying old ways

regime authoritarian rule

republic literally 'rule by the people'

Shanghai Purge attack on Communists by Nationalist forces in Shanghai in 1927 that signalled the start of the long Communist-Nationalist civil war

socialism an ideology that promotes the abolition of private property in favour of rule and ownership of all goods and services by the state

soviet (n.) in China, a Communist base area in the civil war

Soviet (adj.) relating to the people or government of the USSR

Taiwan island in the East China Sea, also known as Formosa, to which Jiang Jieshi's Nationalists retreated after defeat in the civil war

38th Parallel geographical line separating North and South Korea

tributary state a state acknowledging submission to a more powerful one by payment or other means

UN United Nations; an organization set up after World War II to provide a forum for discussion about matters of international importance

unequal treaties a series of 19th-century treaties that China was forced to sign under threat of force with Britain, France, Russia and other countries, conceding special privileges to the citizens of those lands

USSR Union of Soviet Socialist Republics; until its collapse in 1990, a Communist superpower dominated by Russia

warlord in China, a local military commander who took advantage of the collapse of central authority after the revolution of 1911 to seize power in his own region

Index